TUSCANY
AND THE SURROUNDING REGIONS

TUSCAN RECIPES FOR
THE ADVENTUROUS COOK

TUSCANY
AND THE SURROUNDING REGIONS

TUSCAN RECIPES FOR
THE ADVENTUROUS COOK

Quantum
Books

A QUANTUM BOOK

Published by
Quantum Books Ltd
6 Blundell Street
London N7 9BH

1-86160-201-4

Project Manager: Rebecca Kingsley
Designer: Bruce Low
Editor: Sarah Harris

The material in this publication previously appeared in
Italian Regional Cooking,
The Complete Italian Cookbook

QUMTSCN
Set in Fritz Quadrata
Reproduced in Singapore by Eray Scan
Printed in Singapore by Star Standard Industries (Pte) Ltd

Contents

....

INTRODUCTION

Tuscany and the surrounding regions in Italy are home to some of the most distinctive and delicious recipes in the world. The regional variations in the cuisine of this part of Italy stem largely from the fierce sense of local pride that

the inhabitants hold for their traditional dishes. This pride has developed over centuries during which each region remained in relative isolation from its neighbours, both politically and geographically. Indeed, it was only during the latter part of the nineteenth century that the regions were united. Today the diversity of Italian cookery is recognised and enjoyed throughout the world.

One of the main reasons that each region holds its own local dishes so dearly is that a great emphasis is placed on the use of fresh ingredients. With this in mind it is understandable that Italians make the best use of locally grown or raised produce, rather than journeying any distance to obtain ingredients. There is little doubt that fresh foods impart the best flavours, whether this is in the form of home-grown fruits and vegetables, or just-caught fish from the sea.

This respect for food, together with the emphasis placed on the quality of the ingredients is highlighted by one of the main characteristics of Italian cooking.

Unlike French food, for example, which often includes sophisticated sauces, Italian cooking is intended to bring out the natural flavours of the ingredients. It is this that gives the regions of Italy their

reputation for healthy, hearty meals. Home cooking at its best, Italian cuisine offers a varied range of recipes, many of which can be easily mastered by even the most inexperienced chef.

Tuscany and the surrounding regions have a deserved reputation for providing some of the tastiest dishes in Italian cuisine. Wholesome and delicious, as well as filling,

it is easy to understand why the inhabitants of these regions take such delight in their food. Although each region shares the preference for simplicity over sophistication, there are subtle differences between the regions, and each is known for particular specialities.

At the very heart of Italy, Tuscany is famed for its traditional cuisine. In the past, critics have been disdainful of the simplicity of Tuscan dishes, but today rustic cooking is no longer the poor relation in the culinary world. As people have become more health-conscious, the very lack of heavy, complex sauces makes traditional Tuscan fare both healthy and delicious. Beans feature heavily in the cooking of

this region, served in soups and risottos or with tuna as an appetiser. Game is also a staple ingredient, taking advantage of the rich hunting available in the Tuscan hills. In most cases this is simply roasted and lightly seasoned. Spinach is also widely used, leading to the use outside Italy of the culinary term 'alla fiorentina', meaning, with spinach. Any of the Tuscan recipes can be perfectly complemented with the famous wine from this region - Chianti.

The region of Lazio is known for its pasta dishes, featuring a variety of sauces such as alla carrettiera - tuna and mushroom and alla carbonara - bacon, eggs and cream. Pasta ranges from the sheet-based types such as canneloni, favoured in the north of the region, to the tubular pasta more common in the south. Another well-known and popular dish from the Lazio region is Saltimbocca, a dish of ham-topped veal.

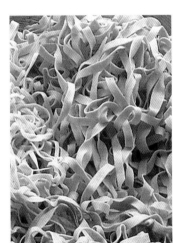

Bologna, in the Emilia-Romagna region to the north-east of Tuscany, is also noted for its fresh pasta, and, of course, its famous spaghetti sauce! This region is one of the richest in terms of the sheer abundance of foods available, due largely to its lush climate and fertile soil. Emilia-Romagna is also home to the mortadella, one of Italy's finest sausages, and parmesan cheese.

The Liguria region, north of Tuscany shares many of its neighbours' priorities in regard to food preparation and cooking. Fish is a strong feature of many dishes, and freshness is of paramount importance. Such is the desire for the freshest possible foods throughout Italy, that fish dishes are served less frequently the further inland you go. This again emphasises the preference within each region for using mainly local ingredients. When there is an abundance of delicious food available close to hand, why bring in ingredients from elsewhere?

The recipes in this book have been selected to bring together the very best dishes from Tuscany and the surrounding regions. To enjoy the full flavour of each dish, it is important that you adopt the Italian approach to cooking, which in simple terms means the ingredients are everything! Choose the freshest cuts of meat and fish, and use fresh herbs where possible, although dried ones will certainly not detract from the taste. If you are lucky enough to be able to grow your own vegetables, this will add an extra touch to that authentic home-cooked flavour. You should also remember that these recipes have been handed down through the generations, and have been adapted

according each cook's preferences and choice. With this in mind, do not be afraid to experiment, by adding or substituting ingredients as you progress. You can be sure that by bringing out the natural taste

and goodness of the ingredients, these recipes will delight the adventurous and the health-conscious alike.

CHAPTER ONE

SOUPS AND STARTERS

JELLIED TOMATO MOUSSE

■

COOKED HAM IN GELATIN

■

BEAN AND VEGETABLE SOUP

■

CRAZY-CUT PASTA
ROMAGNOLA STYLE

JELLIED TOMATO MOUSSE
Mousse di Pomodoro in Gelatina

SERVES 4

INGREDIENTS

450 g (1 lb) tomatoes, peeled, seeded, chopped

Salt

75 ml (2¼ floz) thick béchamel sauce

1 envelope unflavoured gelatin

75 ml (2¼ floz) dry sherry

525 ml (17½ floz) cups beef stock

½ pt whipping cream, whipped

Purée tomatoes in a blender or press through a strainer, season with salt and cook gently for 5 minutes. Put to drain in a cloth tied up at 4 corners over a bowl for 2½ hours. Mix drained tomatoes thoroughly with béchamel sauce; press through a strainer or process in a blender. Refrigerate for 20 minutes. Meanwhile, soften gelatin in sherry. Heat stock in a small pan; add softened gelatin and stir over low heat until completely dissolved. Chill until syrupy and slightly thickened. Pour half the gelatin mixture into a glass bowl and swirl to cover sides. Chill until set (do not refrigerate remaining gelatin mixture). Mix tomato mixture with a wooden spoon to give a soft, smooth consistency. Fold in whipped cream. Spoon into gelatin-coated bowl. If necessary, stir remaining gelatin mixture over low heat until liquefied; then pour over tomato mixture. Chill until set. Unmould onto a serving dish and serve.

COOKED HAM IN GELATIN
Prosciutto Cotto in Gelatina

SERVES 4

INGREDIENTS

8 slices cooked ham

1 envelope unflavoured gelatin

75 ml (2½ floz) dry sherry

525 ml (17½ floz) cups beef stock

Cut ham slices in half and roll them up. Soften gelatin in sherry. Heat stock in a small pan; add softened gelatin and stir over low heat until completely dissolved. Pour a little gelatin into bottom of a dish and refrigerate until set. Arrange ham rolls on gelatin; drizzle remaining gelatin over ham and chill for 2 hours. The ham rolls may also be stuffed with pâté or Russians salad.

BEAN AND VEGETABLE SOUP
Zuppa di Fagiolialla Marchigiana
SERVES 4

INGREDIENTS

30 g (1½ oz) chopped bacon

65 g (2½ oz) dried white beans, soaked

Salt

½ onion

½ stalk celery

½ bunch parsley

Vegetable oil

1 tbsp tomato purée

40 g (1½ oz) chopped green cabbage

40 g (1½ oz) peeled, chopped potato

25 g (1 oz) cauliflowerets

1 bunch beetroots, cooked, peeled, diced

Pepper

65 g (2½ oz) shelled fresh peas

4 slices toast

Blanch bacon, drain and put in a pan with beans. Pour in 2100 ml (3½ pt) water, season with salt, and cook until beans are done. Drain beans and reserve cooking liquid. Meanwhile, chop together onion, celery and parsley and fry in a large pan in a little oil until soft. Add tomato purée diluted with a little water. Pour in bean cooking liquid and stir in cabbage, potato, cauliflower and beetroots. Season with salt and pepper. Simmer soup for 30 minutes, adding more water if necessary.

Meanwhile, purée half the beans and cook peas separately. Add all beans and peas to soup and heat through. Put toast in a soup tureen and pour in the soup. Let it stand for a few minutes before serving.

CRAZY-CUT PASTA ROMAGNOLA STYLE

Malfattini alla Romagnola

SERVES 4

INGREDIENTS

65 g (2½ oz) plain flour

3 eggs, beaten

Salt

Pinch of ground nutmeg

900 ml (1½ pt) chicken or beef stock

Heap flour on work surface, make a well in the middle and add eggs and a pinch of salt and nutmeg. Form into a dough and knead mixture until it is smooth. Form dough into a rectangular loaf shape and leave to dry out a little. Cut it into thick slices and let dry a little longer. Chop coarsely and dry out completely. Pour stock into a pan and bring to the boil. Add pasta and cook for 2–3 minutes, then serve in soup bowls.

CHAPTER TWO

FISH, CHICKEN AND GAME

INGREDIENTS

1 900 g (2 lb) salmon trout (or use a large trout)

2 small carrots, chopped

1 stalk celery, chopped

2 small onions, chopped

1 tbsp chopped parsley

3 medium potatoes, peeled, sliced

4 cloves garlic

2 slices white bread, crusts trimmed, softened in vinegar

Salt and pepper

300 ml (½ pt) vegetable oil

Lemon wedges

12 g (½ oz) butter, melted

SALMON TROUT WITH AÏOLI
Trota Salmonata con Agliata alla Ligure
SERVES 4

Clean and wash trout, put in a fish kettle or a pan that it will fit and cover with a court bouillon made from 1800 ml (3 pt) water, the carrots, celery, onions and parsley. Bring to a gentle boil and simmer for 12 minutes or until fish is done. Boil potatoes in salted water. In a mortar, pound garlic with the bread, season with salt and pepper and gradually add oil, as if you were making mayonnaise. Drain trout, put onto a dish and surround with lemon wedges. Drain potatoes, drizzle with melted butter, and serve with fish; pass aïoli separately.

CHICKEN STUFFED WITH ARTICHOKES

Pollo Ripieno ai Carciofi

SERVES 4

Preheat oven to 180°C/350°F/ gas 4. Crush garlic and rosemary. Put in a bowl with butter, salt and pepper; mix with a wooden spoon until finely creamed. Wash chicken, pat dry and stuff with artichokes and lemon. Sew up opening with cooking thread. Skewer chicken together with a thin skewer, putting 1 sage leaf under each wing and each leg. Rub butter mixture all over chicken, then sprinkle with salt and pepper. Put in a baking pan or dish and pour oil over. Roast for 1½ hours, turning frequently. Remove from oven when golden brown. Transfer to a serving plate and cut into pieces. Arrange artichoke hearts around chicken. Discard lemon. Pour wine into pan and heat over low heat, stirring to blend wine and dripping. Pour sauce over chicken and serve at once.

INGREDIENTS

1 clove garlic

Rosemary sprig

2 tbsp butter

Salt and pepper

1 1¾ kg (about 3 lb) broiler-fryer

4 cooked artichoke hearts

1 lemon, pierced in several places

4 fresh sage leaves

2 tbsp olive oil

About 225 ml (7 floz) dry white wine

FRIED STUFFED SARDINES
Sarde Fritte alla Ligure
SERVES 4

Clean sardines, removing heads and tails. Open them out, remove bones, wash and pat dry. Heat a little olive oil in a frying pan, chop mushrooms finely and fry gently for a few minutes. Transfer them to a dish and add fresh bread crumbs, Parmesan, garlic, oregano, 2 eggs and a pinch of salt. Stuff sardines with this mixture, then close them up. Beat remaining 2 eggs with salt and pepper. Dip stuffed sardines first into flour, then into seasoned beaten egg, then into dry bread crumbs. Fry in hot oil and serve immediately.

INGREDIENTS

16 fresh sardines

Olive oil

2 tbsp dried mushrooms, soaked, drained

1 tbsp fresh bread crumbs, softened in a little milk and squeezed dry

1 tbsp grated Parmesan cheese

1 clove garlic, crushed

1 tsp chopped fresh oregano

Pinch of dried leaf oregano

4 eggs

Salt and pepper

plain flour

Fine dry bread crumbs

RED MULLET WITH HAM
Triglie al Prosciutto

SERVES 4

Clean and scale fish; wash, pat dry and season with salt. Wrap each one in a slice of prosciutto. Peel tomatoes, then seed and slice. Cook garlic for 5 minutes in a pan with some oil. Add mullet and cook for 2–3 minutes on each side, turning them gently. Add tomatoes, sprinkle with bread crumbs, season with salt and pepper and cook over low heat for 10 minutes. Sprinkle with parsley and lemon juice. Put mullet on a dish and serve.

INGREDIENTS

12 small red mullet

Salt

12 slices proscuitto

4 ripe tomatoes

1 clove garlic

Olive oil

25 g (1oz) bread crumbs

Pepper

1 tbsp chopped parsley

Juice of ½ lemon

QUAIL IN BRANDY WITH PEAS
Quaglie al Brandy alla Romana
SERVES 4

Wash quail, pat dry and truss each with a skewer. Melt 25 g (1oz) butter in a pan, put in quail and cook briskly for 15 minutes. Moisten with brandy and let this evaporate almost completely. Transfer quail to a serving dish with cooking juices, remove skewers and keep hot. In a separate pan, fry onion in remaining 25 g (1oz) butter, add peas and a little stock, season with salt and pepper, and cook until tender. Just before removing peas from heat, add prosciutto. Garnish the quail with peas and prosciutto and serve.

INGREDIENTS

8 100-175 g (4-6 oz) quail

50 g (2 oz) butter

About 150 g (5 floz) brandy

½ onion, chopped

65 g (2½ oz) shelled fresh peas

Chicken stock

Salt and freshly ground pepper

225 g (½ lb) prosciutto, cut into strips

SARDINES WITH PEPPER AND TOMATO SAUCE

Sardine Sotto'olio alla Veneta

SERVES 4

Bone sardines carefully and reassemble them on a serving dish. Decorate with the bell pepper and egg whites. Press tomatoes through a strainer and cream with the butter, sage and garlic. Season with salt and pepper and spoon over the sardines.

INGREDIENTS

12 sardines in oil

1 green or red bell pepper, roasted; skinned, cut into strips

Whites of 3 hard-boiled eggs, chopped

65 g (2½ oz) peeled, seeded, chopped tomatoes

2 tbsp butter

Few fresh sage leaves, chopped

1 clove garlic, crushed

Salt and pepper

RED MULLET LIVORNO STYLE
Triglie alla Livornese
SERVES 4

Wash tomatoes, peel and press through a strainer. In a small pan, heat the butter, 2 tablespoons oil and the basil, then add the tomatoes, season with salt and pepper and cook gently for 30 minutes. Meanwhile, clean and scale fish and remove the fins; wash fish and pat dry. Finely chop celery and garlic. Place celery, garlic, parsley and about 75 ml (2½ floz) oil into pan which you can bring to the table. Fry for a few minutes. Lightly flour the fish and brown on one side. Remove from the heat and very carefully (mullet are fragile) turn them over. Put them back on the heat. Pour over the tomato sauce and cook for about 10 minutes. Serve fish in the pan.

INGREDIENTS

450 g (1 lb) ripe tomatoes

2 tbsp butter

Olive oil

Few fresh basil leaves, chopped

Salt and pepper

4 red mullet or 225 g (½ lb) redfish

1 stalk celery

1 clove garlic

25 g (1 oz) chopped parsley

Plain flour

CHAPTER THREE

MEAT DISHES

Veal Kidneys with Mushrooms

■

Genoese Meatballs

■

Potroast Beef with Cinnamon

■

Veal scallops with Ham

■

Tuscan Veal with Ham

■

Steak with Gorgonzola Butter

■

Lamb and Artichoke Casserole

■

Ham Slices with anchovy sauce

■

Pork Chops with Olives

VEAL KIDNEYS WITH MUSHROOMS

Rognone di Vitello al Tegame con Funghi

SERVES 4

Fry onion and garlic in oil, add mushrooms, season with salt and pepper and cook through over medium heat. In another frying pan, sauté kidneys in half the butter and a few tablespoons oil until done. Season, add mushroom mixture and cook briefly. Put on a serving dish, sprinkle with parsley and garnish with bread cut into triangles and fried in remaining butter and a little oil.

INGREDIENTS

1 tbsp chopped onion
1 clove garlic, crushed
Vegetable oil
4 fresh mushrooms, sliced
Salt and pepper
225 g (½ lb) veal kidneys, fat and skin removed
12 g (½ oz) butter
Chopped parsley
2 slices bread

35

GENOESE MEATBALLS
Polpette alla Genovese
SERVES 4

INGREDIENTS

150 g (3 oz) ground cooked veal

3 tbsp fresh bread crumbs, soaked in stock

or milk and squeezed dry

1 clove garlic, crushed

1 bunch parsley, chopped

Few fresh oregano leaves

2 tbsp dried mushrooms, soaked, drained,

chopped

2 tbsp grated Parmesan cheese

Salt and pepper

Ground nutmeg

1 egg, beaten

Plain flour

Vegetable oil

Solid vegetable shortening

In a bowl, mix the veal, bread crumbs, garlic, parsley, oregano, mushrooms and cheese. Season with salt, pepper and nutmeg; blend in egg, mixing well. Form mixture into balls, flatten slightly and dip in flour. Brown quickly in plenty of oil and shortening, then reduce heat and continue to fry until cooked through. Serve hot.

POT-ROAST BEEF WITH CINNAMON

Arrosto di Manzo alla Cannella

SERVES 4

INGREDIENTS

3 onions, thickly sliced

6 tbsp butter

2 tbsp vegetable oil

800 g (1¾ lb) boneless beef chuck roast

Salt and pepper

Pinch of ground cinnamon

Juice of 1 lemon

300 ml (10 floz) dry white wine

1 bay leaf

Put onions into a pan with butter and oil. Cook over low heat for 5 minutes. Add meat; sprinkle with salt, pepper and cinnamon. Pour in lemon juice and wine, add bay leaf, cover and cook over low heat for 2½ hours, turning meat every so often. When meat is tender, remove from pan, slice and arrange on a serving dish. Pour over the hot sauce from the pan and serve.

VEAL SCALLOPS WITH HAM
Saltimbocca alla Romana
SERVES 4

8 veal cutlets (saltimbocca)

Salt and pepper

8 slices of prosciutto

8 fresh sage leaves

Plain flour

5 tbsp butter

150 ml (5 floz) dry white wine

Flatten veal cutlets and sprinkle with salt and pepper. Cover each cutlet with a slice of prosciutto and a sage leaf, then fold each one in half and secure with a skewer. Flour lightly. Heat 4 tablespoons butter in a frying pan and fry saltimbocca over medium-high heat until brown all over and cooked through. Remove with a slotted spoon and arrange on a serving dish. Add wine to cooking juices and reduce almost completely. Add remaining 1 tablespoon butter and stir until melted; pour hot sauce over saltimbocca. Serve at once.

TUSCAN VEAL WITH HAM
Vitello con Prosciutto alla Toscana
SERVES 4

Season meat with salt and pepper and flour lightly. Melt butter in a heavy saucepan, add a little oil and brown meat. Stir in onion and prosciutto, pour in wine and cook over high heat until liquid is almost evaporated. Cover meat with water and continue to cook, turning meat occasionally. Just before veal is done, add potatoes and stir in garlic, lemon peel and nutmeg; let flavours mingle. Put meat on a serving dish, pour over cooking juices, surround with potatoes and serve.

INGREDIENTS

1 900 g (2 lb) veal rump roast
Salt and pepper
Plain flour
3 tbsp butter
Vegetable oil
1 onion, chopped
100 g (¼ lb) prosciutto, cut into strips
300 ml (10 floz) dry red wine
2 medium potatoes, boiled, peeled, cut into chunks
1 clove garlic, minced
Grated peel of 1 lemon
Ground nutmeg

STEAK WITH GORGONZOLA BUTTER
Bistecche di Manzo con Burrodi Gorgonzola
SERVES 4

INGREDIENTS

6 tbsp butter

25 g (1 oz) crumbled mild gorgonzola cheese

1 tbsp chopped parsley

Lemon juice

4 100 g (4 oz) tender steaks

Salt and pepper

Put 4 tablespoons butter, the gorgonzola, parsley and a few drops of lemon juice into a bowl and beat with a wooden spoon until mixture is smooth and creamy. Roll mixture into a cylinder and wrap in foil. Refrigerate for 1 hour. Melt remaining 2 tablespoons butter in a pan, add steaks and cook over high heat for 2 minutes on each side. Drain, season with salt and pepper and put on a serving dish. Cut gorgonzola butter into 12 slices and put 3 slices on each steak. Serve at once.

LAMB AND ARTICHOKE CASSEROLE
Ragu di Agnello ai Carciofi

SERVES 4

INGREDIENTS

675 g (1½ lb) lean boneless lamb (leg or shoulder), cubed

50 g (2 oz) butter

Vegetable oil

Salt and pepper

Chicken stock

8 cooked artichoke hearts

150 ml (5 floz) dry white wine

Chopped parsley

Brown meat in 5 tablespoons butter and a little oil, season with salt and pepper and cook over low heat until tender, adding stock as necessary. Cut artichoke hearts into strips and cook in remaining 3 tablespoons butter with a pinch of salt. Put lamb onto a dish, add wine to cooking juices and reduce. Pour onto lamb, garnish with artichokes, sprinkle with parsley and serve.

HAM SLICES WITH ANCHOVY SAUCE

Prosciutto Fresco di Maiale Salsato

SERVES 4

INGREDIENTS

8 75 g (3 oz) slices ham

Pepper

Plain flour

2 eggs, beaten

Few tablespoons fresh bread crumbs

7 tbsp butter

1 small onion, chopped

5 flat anchovy fillets, rinsed well, mashed

1 tbsp capers, chopped

1 tbsp chopped parsley

Vinegar

Chicken stock

Flatten ham slices with a mallet and season with pepper; then dip in flour, egg and bread crumbs. Melt 2 tablespoons butter in a pan, add onion and cook over low heat until soft. Add anchovy fillets, capers, parsley, 1 tablespoon flour and a little pepper. Stir over a high heat for a few minutes; stir in 2–3 tablespoons vinegar and let evaporate. Add enough stock to give a slightly thickened sauce. Dice 1 tablespoon butter and stir into sauce a piece at a time, making sure that each piece is fully incorporated before adding the next. Keep warm. In a separate pan, melt remaining 4 tablespoons butter; add breaded ham slices and brown on both sides, then reduce heat and cook for 10–12 minutes, turning occasionally. Arrange on a serving dish, pour over sauce and serve accompanied with buttered spinach.

PORK CHOPS WITH OLIVES
Costolette di Maiale alle Olive

SERVES 4

Peel 18 cloves of garlic; cook for 3 minutes in boiling water, then drain. Flatten chops and insert remaining garlic, cut into slivers. Prepare a marinade with oil, a little vinegar, rosemary, sage, salt and pepper. Put chops in marinade and let stand for 2 hours, turning occasionally. Drain and pat dry. Boil olives in water and cover for 10 minutes, remove from heat and keep hot in cooking liquid. Heat shortening in a pan with 1 tablespoon oil and add chops; brown for 3 minutes on each side. Reduce heat, add drained garlic and continue to cook for 12 minutes longer or until chops are cooked through, turning occasionally. Put chops on a plate and pile garlic and drained olives in the centre. Pour marsala or wine into pan juices and reduce slightly; simmer for 5 minutes, then pour sauce onto the chops. Sprinkle with chopped parsley and serve.

INGREDIENTS

20 cloves garlic

4 pork chops

Vegetable oil

Vinegar

Rosemary sprigs

Few fresh sage leaves

Salt and pepper

40 g (1½ oz) large green olives

1 tbsp solid vegetable shortening

75 ml (2½ floz) marsala or white wine

75 ml (2½ floz) condensed beef bouillon

1 tbsp chopped parsley

CHAPTER FOUR

PASTA AND PRIMI PIATTI

RAVIOLI WITH SAGE AND PUMPKIN
Ravioli alla Salvia con la Zucca
SERVES 4

Preheat oven to 200°C/400°F/gas 6 . For the pasta, follow instructions on pp.58–59, mixing a pinch of salt with the flour. For the filling, bake pumpkin until tender and scrape flesh into a bowl. Mash pumpkin well. Stir in parmesan, amaretti cookies, and the mustard. Season with salt, pepper and a pinch of nutmeg and mix well. To prepare ravioli, place filling at 5–6½ cm intervals. Boil ravioli in plenty of salted water until al dente. Drain and arrange in layers in a baking dish, topping each layer with melted, browned butter, sage and parmesan. Finish with a sprinkling of parmesan. Bake in oven until golden brown.

INGREDIENTS

For the pasta
450 g (1 lb) plain flour
Salt
5 eggs
1 tsp vegetable oil

For the filling
2 kg (4¼ lb) pumpkin, seeded
50 g (2 oz) grated parmesan cheese
4 crushed amaretti biscuits
Coarse-grained mustard, or Italian fruity mustard, if available
Salt and pepper
Pinch of ground nutmeg

For the sauce
75 ml (2½ floz) melted, browned butter
Few fresh sage leaves, chopped
35 g (1½ oz) grated parmesan cheese

INGREDIENTS

600 g (24 oz) plain flour

Vegetable oil

Salt

900 g (2 lb) sorrel

50 g (2 oz) grated parmesan cheese

Dried Leaf oregano

9 eggs

Pepper

175g (7 oz) ricotta cheese

SORREL AND EGG PIE
Torta Pasqualina
SERVES 4

Pour flour onto a board and make a well in the centre. Mix in 2 tablespoons oil, a pinch of salt and enough lukewarm water to give a dough of same consistency as for homemade pasta (see p. 58-59). Knead for 10 minutes. Divide into 14 pieces and shape each one into a ball. Dust with flour, cover and let stand for an hour. Preheat oven to 200°C/400°F/gas 6. Wash sorrel, discarding any discoloured leaves and large stalks. Put it in a pan with only the water clinging to it, cover and cook gently over low heat, stirring occasionally to make sure it does not stick to pan. When sorrel is cooked (about 8 minutes), squeeze out water, then chop sorrel and place in a bowl. Add 25 g (1 oz) cup parmesan, a pinch of oregano, 3 eggs and the ricotta. Season mixture with salt and pepper, then mix well. Roll out one of the pastry balls very thinly and lay on a greased baking sheet. Sprinkle it with a few drops of oil. Roll out a second pastry ball and lay it on top of the first. Continue rolling, oiling and stacking the pastry balls until you have 7 layers. Put sorrel filling on top. Make 6 dents with back of a spoon and into each break an egg. Season and sprinkle with remaining 25 g (1 oz) parmesan. Roll out other 7 balls until very thin and lay them on top, greasing each one with oil. Prick top sheet with a fork, brush with a little oil and bake in oven for an hour. Allow to cool and serve cold.

SPINACH TORTELLONI BAKE
Tortelloni con Pasta Verde al Gratin

SERVES 4

For the pasta, follow instructions on pages. 58–59. For the filling, thoroughly mix all filling ingredients together. Cut out the pasta, fill and shape into tortelloni (see illustrations 1 and 2 on page 58). For the sauce, cook onion in oil until softened, stir in tomatoes and basil leaves and season with salt and pepper. Cook the tortelloni in boiling salted water until al dente. Layer the tortelloni in a buttered baking dish; dot each layer with butter, sprinkle with parmesan and spread with tomato sauce. Finish with a layer of mozzarella cheese and put into a hot oven until the cheese melts. Serve hot.

INGREDIENTS

For the pasta
230 g (9½ oz) cups all-purpose flour
225 g (½ lb) fresh spinach, cooked, puréd, thoroughly drained
4 eggs

For the filling
150 g (6 oz) ricotta cheese
450 g (1 lb) fresh spinach, cooked, puréed, thoroughly drained
50 g (2 oz) chopped prosciutto
3 tbsp grated parmesan cheese
1 egg yolk
Pinch of ground nutmeg
Salt and pepper

For the sauce
1 small onion, chopped
2 tbsp olive oil
75 g (3 oz) sieved tomatoes
Chopped fresh basil leaves
Salt and pepper
25 g (1 oz) butter
3 tbsp grated parmesan cheese
Sliced mozzarella cheese

RICE WITH HAM AND CHICKEN LIVERS
Risotto alla Trasteverina
SERVES 4

Fry onion in 2½ tablespoons butter, add pancetta, season with salt and pepper and cook gently for 2 minutes. Add marsala or red wine and let it evaporate almost completely. Stir in livers and prosciutto. Add rice and ladle on stock gradually as rice absorbs it, stirring constantly. Remove risotto from heat, stir in remaining 2½ tablespoons butter and a little parmesan. Leave to stand for 1 minute, then serve sprinkled with remaining 2½ tablespoons parmesan.

INGREDIENTS

½ small onion, finely chopped

5 tbsp butter, diced

50 g (2 oz) diced lean pancetta bacon

Salt and pepper

150 g (5 floz) dry marsala *or* red wine

50 g (2 oz) sliced chicken livers

50 g (2 oz) julienne-cut prosciutto

350 g (14 oz) cups rice

Chicken or beef stock

5 tbsp grated parmesan cheese

Tortellini and Tortelloni

Prepare as right and roll out. Cover pasta with a cloth to avoid drying out, except in area where you are working. There are two basic tortellini shapes: square – like ravioli – and curved triangles with joined edges. When these are large and served as a first course in sauce instead of in a broth, they are often called tortelloni. Below is a simple version of tortelloni verde al gratin.

Place a nut-sized piece of filling – either meat or ricotta and spinach – towards one corner of a square of pasta

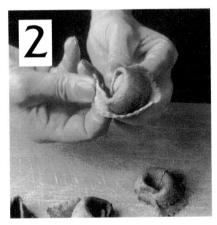

Fold the top over to form a triangle and join the points together to make a curved shape

HOMEMADE PASTA
Pasta Fatta in Casa

serves 4

Dust work surface with flour. Mound flour onto board and make a well in the centre. Break eggs into it. Add 1 tablespoon cold water to eggs and 1 or 2 teaspoons oil. Beat eggs with fork and gradually work in flour, using your hands when the dough becomes stiff. Knead for at least 10 minutes. Dough should be stiff – add extra flour if it is too soft. When little air bubbles start to appear, roll dough into a ball, flatten then roll out with a rolling pin as far as possible, making sure that the thickness is uniform,

RAVIOLI

Make pasta dough as above, roll pasta into a sheet, dot with filling, and topping with a second sheet cut and into squares.

INGREDIENTS

5 tbsp butter, diced
450 g (1 lb) plain flour
4 medium eggs
vegetable oil

INGREDIENTS

450 g (2 lb) fresh spinach

Vegetable oil

1 clove garlic, crushed

25 g (1 oz) finely diced bacon

32 tbsp pine nuts

3 tbsp golden raisins, soaked in lukewarm
water until plump

Salt

Butter

SPINACH ROMAN STYLE
Spinaci alla Romana

SERVES 4

Wash spinach, discarding tough stalks and discoloured leaves. Cook gently in water clinging to leaves, then drain and squeeze dry. Heat a little oil in a pan, add garlic, bacon and spinach, and cook, gently stirring. After a few minutes, add pine nuts and golden raisins. Remove from heat, season with salt, put in a serving dish, top with about 1 tablespoon butter and serve.

COUNTRY-STYLE PEPPERS AND TOMATOES

Rusticana alla Piacentina

SERVES 4

Heat butter with some oil in a pan and fry the green onions and peppers until half cooked. If desired you may roast and peel peppers before sautéing with onions. Then add tomatoes, season with salt, add a little lukewarm water and cook over medium heat, stirring occasionally. As soon as peppers are cooked, stir in eggs and serve.

INGREDIENTS

25 g (1 oz) butter

Vegetable oil

450 g (1 lb) green onions

4 large greens or yellow bell peppers, seeded, cut into strips

450 g (1 lb) tomatoes, peeled, seeded, chopped

Salt

4 hard-boiled eggs, chopped

NEW ONIONS ESCOFFIER

Cipolline Novelle alla Escoffier

SERVES 4

INGREDIENTS

800 g (1¾ lb) small white onions

Vegetable oil

Salt and pepper

1 bay leaf

Pinch of dried leaf thyme

1 tsp fennel seeds

3 tbsp golden raisins, soaked in lukewarm
water until plump

150 ml (5 floz) dry white wine

About 75 ml (2½ floz) Cognac

Peel onions and boil for 5 minutes. Drain and pat dry. Heat some oil in a pan, add onions, season with salt and pepper and fry gently until golden brown, being careful not to let them burn. Add bay leaf, thyme, fennel seeds and golden raisins, and pour in wine and cognac. Bring to a boil, cover and cook for 5 minutes longer. Remove from the heat, allow to cool and serve.